C000069761

life interrupted
d.l. heather

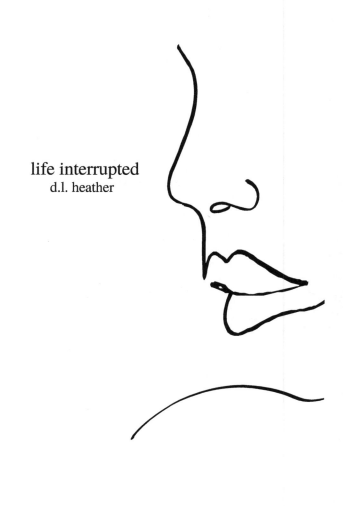

also by d.l. heather

metamorphosis
petals of healing
metamorphosis - extended edition

ISBN: 9780473511289

this book is for all my fellow endo warriors
with love

10% of the proceeds from *life interrupted* will be
donated to endometriosis research

table of contents

I was 39 when I finally had endometriosis related surgery. I was hoping to finally have some answers, but also terrified that they may find nothing at all. My stomach was in knots and the surgical nurses could see how anxious I was, and began squeezing my shaky hands, saying, "you're going to be just fine." For 25 years, I suffered from debilitating pain, which consumed me to where I thought it was only going to end in one of two ways. Either whatever it was inside me causing all this pain was going to kill me or I would eventually take my own life. I had been to countless appointments, dismissed, and misdiagnosed nearly every time. Finally, after 4.5 hours of surgery, I woke up to my surgeon reassuring me that for two- and-a-half decades of inaction, my pain was indeed real and she confirmed I had adenomyosis and stage 4 endometriosis.

I can still remember, when my childhood friends got their first periods, they appeared to celebrate the momentous occasion because they were blossoming into young women. I never felt that way, though. When I was 12, I had my first period and when it was my time to blossom, it was pure agony.

Since day one, I experienced heavy bleeding and crippling pain from what I used to describe as being stabbed with jagged serrated knives twisting and turning into my abdomen, sides, lower back, pelvis and ovaries. At 14, after several doctors' appointments, they prescribed birth control, which brought on anxiety, depression, and severe nausea. At 15, my doctor suggested I seek counseling after telling me my pain must be all in my head, "You're too young to have all this pain you're describing" and upon my first visit with the counselor she asked, "Why do you think you're experiencing this pain? "Tell me about your home life." I sat there stunned, and at that point, began questioning my sanity.

My anxiety deepened and clung to me every time I told doctors about the pain through the years. I had trips to the emergency room far too often because I could barely get out of bed on the days leading up to menstruating, during, and after. I saw three different gynecologists in a year where I was probed and prodded each time. I observed them as they read my file, and I knew what they were thinking. I couldn't help but feel like I was a lost cause, wondering if the doctors were right.

Was my pain all in my head?
Was I an attention seeker?

With every year that passed, the pain became worse and during the bad days; I was in the fetal position bawling and clutching my stomach. I was seeing my doctor on average two to three times a week begging for blood tests, ultrasounds, or at least something to ease my pain. Each time, they would tell me it was just thrush or a UTI. Prescribed a cocktail of Ibuprofen, Tylenol, and/or Panadol for the pain along with some vaginal cream and sent me on my merry way. I would return a few days later, still in unbearable pain, and would leave with zero help. During several visits, my doctor would typically say: "I'm sensing a feeling of frustration from you." I was being stripped to my core and my body was medicalized in every way. On days where the pain became unmanageable, I sat in the hospital waiting room for four to six hours. Every time it was the same. Rate the pain, take off my clothes, be prodded to locate the pain, get blood work done, take an anti-inflammatory. Everything looked normal. By the time I was 18, I had rehearsed every question and answer before even going to the hospital. The fatigue, anger, and frustration wore me down.

As a young woman presenting pelvic pain in the emergency room, I felt devalued by our health system. Nearly every time being met with doubt when describing the intensity of my pain. Given the severity of my discomfort, I would rate my pain 10/10 most times and on more than one occasion, was told by a nurse: "I don't think you understand the rating system, a 10/10 would be like the pain is so bad you feel as if you're going to pass out or die." I was told that I was too sensitive and had a low threshold for pain. I've had ER doctors accuse me of being a pill seeker.

Endometriosis is a condition riddled with power struggles in the relationship between patients and their doctors. We're probed and prodded rather than listened to. The results are patients suffering in silence and doubting themselves when blood tests, urine cultures, PAP smears, and ultrasounds all come back normal. Throughout my journey with endometriosis, I have frequently questioned myself because of this, and as I grew older, I would try to hide my emotions during appointments to not appear to be too resentful and emotional, but that's what medical gaslighting does.

My experience with endometriosis has been a constant fight to be seen and heard in the medical community, whether I was living in Canada, the United States or New Zealand. This condition has followed me all my life and is part of who I am, but I no longer let it define me. On 18 October 2019, excision surgery confirmed my diagnosis, but my story is just one amongst the millions of unheard stories around the world. Through writing this book, I hope I can shed some light on the need to recognize the experiences of the one in ten who feel left out by the medical community.

After being diagnosed, treatment has continued to be challenging. Just eight months after my surgery, I had a hysterectomy to remove adenomyosis and had more endometriosis lesions removed. Following that surgery, I developed severe hip, tissue and joint problems and mobility has been a daily struggle. I have recently been diagnosed with fibromyalgia, lupus, interstitial cystitis, and chronic fatigue syndrome too. Every day is a struggle and despite it all, I still have hope for a cure and will continue to fight for us to be heard.

part 1

that first ache
entirely unannounced
she lay still
looking at the sacred crimson
steadily trickling down her thigh

weeping instantly shaming her body

she slowly begins to
wax and wane
just like the moon
the lining of the uterus
needs to shed
before it can rebuild itself
coming back
renewed

she wonders if
she'll always feel ashamed
of its mess and impurity
this nutrient-rich blood flow
that heavily drips between her thighs
the same drip that
causes her crippling pain every month
maybe one day she'll see it
as the gift of womanhood
and not a curse

early on she becomes
embarrassed
by the immature boys
who seem repulsed
by the fact
that she bleeds

the ones that whisper
laugh and look
when she rushes out of
5th period English class with
bloodstained covered pants
dodging all the lurking faces
as she charges through the hallway

she can only handle so much

for years
we've been
conditioned
to feel
this shame
this embarrassment
by a world that treats
MENSTRUATION
like the plague

not again
grieving body
she bleeds
with sorrow

born with a prescription
carved into her stomach
she awoke aching, again
her pelvis ripping her apart
physically drained
emotionally numb

a 14-year-old girl sits scared
she anxiously waits for hours
as the white coats pass by

eventually they begrudgingly examine her
one of them sighs while scanning her chart
the other looks at her
like she's just another number

every dismissive word
shot her way
pierces through like daggers
tearing into her soul

life interrupted

what is a young girl meant to do
when nobody takes her suffering seriously?

not her family
her friends
her doctors

Not One Person

she cradles her aching belly
while fighting back the tears
she gets ready for school
brushes her hair
frantically searches her closet
hoping to find the darkest pair of pants she owns

she grins and bares it
as the words
she's heard far too often
unforgivingly
float around in her head

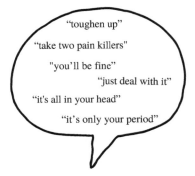

opened mouthed and powerless

she is silent

life interrupted

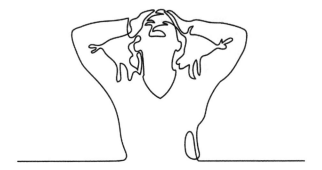

blood on the bathroom floor again
legs uncrossed, she's ashamed
as the stream of steady river
flows between her legs

maybe in time
she'll learn
to love herself

some days she can feel it coming
other days she sits
patiently waiting
for that bastard to resurface

without fail
eventually rearing its ugly head
hitting her with incorrigible spasms
ones so fierce
they hurl her down to the ground
mixed with hormonal imbalances
a rock hard bulging belly
and a vagina that feels like its been trapped
in the epicentre of a forest fire

she hates and loves everything around her

all the noise we make
the suffering we endure
at times keeps us at a distance

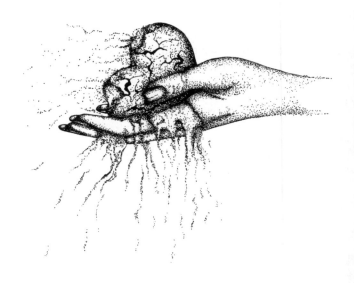

tongues become the sharpest swords
as they slash their way
through your heart

the first time she heard the words
"you're too young for it to be anything serious"
felt like she had been

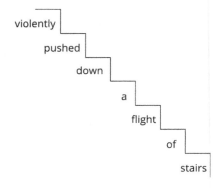

torn down
dismissed, belittled
once again
she's pulled apart by
medical gaslighting

their words are venom
coursing through her veins

exhausted from
the insomnia
the pain
the anxiety

sometimes
the easiest
least draining action
is a pretend smile

faking it

the darkness sits heavy on her chest
blank eyes turn to hollow stares
rigid, losing grip
pushing the limits of her body
just so she appears
NORMAL

life interrupted

there are days
where she can't help but think
she's making herself sick
absorbing all this negative energy
its gravitational pull
is just
too powerful for her to resist

a
  beautiful
      broken
         mess

part 2

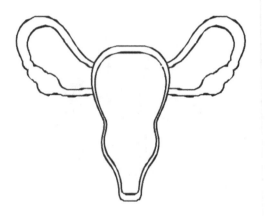

a patient of chaos
closets filled with mirrors
full-mouthed and powerful
she wants the truth
released into the world
where it exists
somewhere other than her body
so she no longer
has to feel

so heavy

day and night
she dreams of a
problem-free vagina
a uterus that doesn't scream back at her
instead; she was granted
an all-encompassing
pile of raging weeds
spreading
refusing
to
bloom

there have been times
where it feels as though
she may win this battle
reducing her daily medication
exercising again
then out of the blue,
this internal light switch
flips off
and suddenly
a pool of heat rises in her pelvis
her organs swell
pushing against her diaphragm

she struggles to breathe

we have stigmas

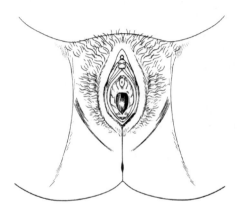

between our thighs

surviving

in a body that

exists on the margins

her body is a battlefield
covered in wounds that run
as deep as the ocean

an overflow of emotions
drag her across desert roads
roads where only wild horses
take refuge

her pain is so great that
she can't shake it, focus
or think of anything else
on these days
she can feel herself fading
slipping away
from this life
just as her father did

perhaps she is
the antagonistic protagonist
in this part of her story

behind her eyes
lies a hidden mystery
a mask she bears
to disguise the pain

when she says, *'I'm fine"*
what does she mean?
no, her pain didn't just evaporate
no, the surgery didn't miraculously cure her
her pain is 24/7
like the sun
never truly going down
rising and falling

medication that
doesn't fix it
this pain is bound to her
even now as she's sitting next to you
her smile never fading
but you don't want to hear the truth
and she's too sick and tired of explaining
that's why she says, *"I'm fine"*

a silence manifests within
as she has adapted to
the changes in her life
a mind like a mirror

always reflecting

how is
she not radiant
having suffered
for so long

falling star

like faded words
that sit on sun-drenched
crinkled pieces of paper
she is distant
tired of living
in a body that's against her

there are days
where it feels
like the world
keeps moving forward
as time stands still
for her
the one in ten
sealed away
in a perpetual prison
waiting to be free

she paces in circles
through suffocating darkness
mouth closed over muffled screams
frustrated that after all this time
nobody can see her pain

what's your pain
on a scale of
one to ten?

to this day
these words
haunt her

endometriosis

(en-do-me-tri-os-is)
noun

a rabid hungry weed
smothering flowers
that were meant
to blossom

imagine having the flu every single day of your life
nausea, aches, pain, anxiety, brain fog
fatigue that comes on like the snap of a finger

strained relationships
canceled plans
sliding in and out of depression

now imagine living that life
but
with symptoms that are continually dismissed
because of society's lack of education

drama queen, attention seeker she has heard it all

imagine pleading with doctors for years
to listen to your cries
to take your suffering seriously
your soul depleted and tired
the burden so heavy

silence becomes your security blanket
that's what it feels like to suffer like her

and the millions of other victims of medical gaslighting

she wonders if your body screams as
loud as hers
she'll never know
because
you don't talk about it
none of us do
we suck it up
pretend everything is fine
only
she wants to spill out her soul
because the breakdown of our bodies
the walking on eggshells
the self-denial
is anything but FINE

it's hard to be
the best version of herself
while dragging a mountain
of resentment
along behind her

for years
she has lived in a vacuum of blinding pain
her uterus feels like the sting
of a thousand diving wasps
her belly, swollen, hard and aching
her pelvis, twitching, contracting and burning
day and night she suffers

a series of bad days
if only she could see
past the pain
beyond the crashing waves
if only she could sleep
through just one night

if only

scalding hot baths

heating pads

pain meds

pads

acupressure mat

tampons

essential oils   pelvic floor therapy

TENS Machine

CBD

ice packs

injections

forced smiles

her daily survival kit filled with golden tools

perhaps if you could see the scars etched deep
into her skin
if they were still raw, jagged, and blood-soaked
scabs falling to the floor

maybe if the stabbing sensations
looked more violent
if the spasms screamed out louder
and if you could feel
the fire burning in her pelvis
or the swelling in her belly

perhaps if the deep shooting pains
were tiny threads of silver
glowing in the sunlight, for all to see
maybe if you took your hand and touched
her skin, you could feel the heaviness
of that light touch

perhaps if the constant sorrow one day took over
the chronic fatigue devouring her whole
and she disappeared like a cloud of smoke

maybe then you would believe her

an inferno infiltrates her pelvis
lesions spread throughout her body
binding organs in places
they were not meant to be
like unwanted weeds
no matter
how deep you reap
the
roots
remain

the constant chatter
of her thoughts and emotions
are devitalizing

it's hard to remember
a time when
she wasn't
broken down to a
one in ten statistic

desperate and looking for answers
she types her symptoms into *google*:

abdominal bloating   irregular periods
      severe back pain   pelvic pressure
      intense cramping   contractions
                 infertility   heavy bleeding
      painful urination   painful sex
             ovarian cysts   chronic fatigue
             burning pelvis   ovulation pain
                rectal pain   sharp, stabbing pain
                    nausea   fist size blood clots
               back and pelvic spasms

one
recurring
word

endometriosis

this bitter taste of black coffee
sits on the roof of her mouth
the distastefulness
swirling around her tongue
as she tries to remember
the last time
she didn't taste such bitterness

maybe she's just unlucky
life interrupted
twisting aching, stabbing pain
unhinged cramps, inflammation
this disease is unforgiving
tearing apart everything in its path

stitch mark after stitch mark
scar lines with a story
remind her of how far
she has come
but some days
darkness takes over the light
and she feels jilted

jailed by her memories

there is no leaving it behind
no brushing it off
even after excision
traces remain
like a brutal breakup
you carry her with you
to work
to school
while running errands
your friends don't understand
they think you've become
distracted, boring
annoying to be around
one by one

       they

          drift

              away

this puddle of grief
strains her soul
and still she
fights
surviving
another day

a bedside drawer full of hospital bands
her collection of unanswered cries
white twisted plastic strips; a reminder
of every time she begged
to be heard

for us, our lives are disrupted
placed on hold, as we fight to exist
hoping for a better day to come
battling on, waiting for a cure

lost in translation
jumbled forgotten words
fog spiraling around her head
starving for recollection

between agony and seduction
heavy periods, ruptured cysts
blood clotting and mood swings
he cuts her down to pieces

intense pain deep like a knife
carving away at her insides
with every penetration
embarrassed and defeated
she waits for this
unresolved trauma to end

like a thief in the night
you've taken away so much

she glances up and sees the face staring back at her
that look; the one she's grown accustomed to
well worn indented lines mark her fierce scowl
just when she thought she was rid of you
as if the memories, trauma, and scars you
inflicted on her weren't enough
but
you've returned
and it's a bitter pill to swallow

endometriosis
is putting a smile on your face
when all you want to do is cry
it's explaining that there is NO cure
it's excruciating pain from head to toe
it's guilt
depression
sadness and shame

it's fighting a daily battle with your body
grappling for some kind of quality of life
it's having things you love taken away from you

canceled plans, losing friends
countless trips to the hospital
medication and multiple surgeries

it's barely holding on

the beast within her
never giving up
flaring through her broken body
ripping apart her insides

sufferers, do not seek attention
NO it's not just a bad period
endo is a cellular monstrous disease

spreading through our bodies like cancer

part 3

invisible illness
cabinet full of pills
a cycle of unawareness
unspoken words
heavy breath, forced silence

she *SHOUTS* as loud
as her lungs will allow
so that one day
years from now
the one in ten
will not have to fight so hard
wondering when their
VOICES will be heard

curled up, knees to chest
cheek pressed against ice cold bathroom tiles
finding the courage to peel herself
back up once again
clenching her stomach
clawing her way to her bed
four walls closing in

she is a warrior

one in ten have
the strength
wounded hearts

lifting roots

life interrupted

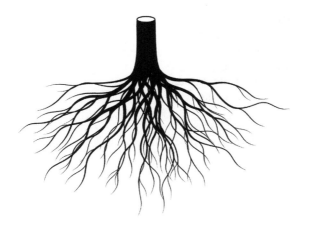

she absorbs her losses
never fully healing
their remains are
a part of her now
a piece of her existence
shaping her into a
stronger
braver
version of herself

for years twisted thoughts
of shame and denial
have put her in a shadowed box
but she will continue to fight
moving freely around
in every darkened corner

looking back at her reflection
learning to love her body
she softly whispers
you are
so much
braver
than you know

this malevolent force
gnaws at her insides
but here she is
in spite of it all

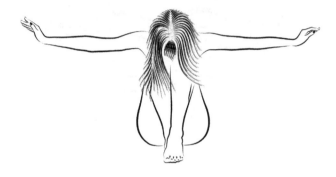

there are days
where she doesn't feel courageous
but still, she carries on
that internal wind
pulls her out of a darkened state
telling her to keep moving
and no matter how hard
the wind tries to pull her back down

she has the strength to be in the present

scars will fade in time
your skin will become part of your story
those sunflowers you planted
last autumn will grow
springtime will circle round again
your wounds will heal

when you've been stuck in
the darkest of places
and everything
fucking hurts
you sometimes
tend to think
you've been buried
deep into the ground
but
perhaps
you've been
planted to grow

morning mist
as always
a smile

rediscovery

she enters
painting
new colors

discovering new light

seeds will grow in total darkness

planted in fertile soil, kept in the dark
and nurtured with water
a seed transforms itself into something beautiful
it creates its way from
the unmanifested and unseen
to the manifested and seen

the seed continues to grow both in the soil,
creating strong roots and above the ground
expressing;

its divine beauty

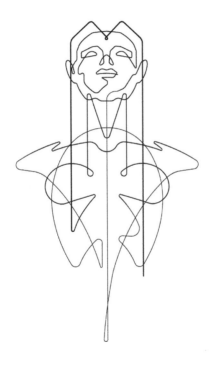

dazzling the sunlight
with her reflection
she gently whispers to her body
please, please stay in this moment
where the pain is manageable

hush the roaring doubt
forget the weight
of the world's opinions
listen to the unwavering
voice within

we are so fragile yet;
so fierce

no matter how dark the night
in the morning new light filters in
covering every corner of the darkness

Lightning Source UK Ltd.
Milton Keynes UK
UKHW020627230223
417504UK00011B/1458

9 780473 511289